AnatoME

The Journey of Puzzled Emotions

Angel Dsouza

BookLeaf
Publishing

Presentation by *BookLeaf Publishing*

Web: www.bookleafpub.com

E-mail: info@bookleafpub.com

ISBN: 9789363307391

First edition 2024

For my Mumma

***Step into the labyrinth of the human heart
and mind with AnatoME:***

The Journey of Puzzled Emotions. This unique interactive book blends poetry, microfiction, and art to guide you through the complex landscape of your feelings. Designed to be more than just a read, AnatoME invites you on a transformative journey of self-discovery and emotional reflection.

Embark on a four-level adventure that begins in the shadows of darkness, confusion, and sadness. Each level is a piece of a larger puzzle, gradually leading you toward light and joy. Through evocative poetry and stirring microfiction, you'll explore the depths of your emotions, confronting and embracing each one.
You will get a chance to reflect on your feelings, reminisce about past experiences, and express your innermost thoughts through journaling. Thought-provoking prompts and beautiful illustrations accompany your journey, encouraging introspection and personal growth.

As you progress, this book evolves into a sanctuary of happiness and tranquillity, where you can reconnect with your inner child. The final pieces of the puzzle come together, offering clarity and peace through creative expression and thoughtful reflection.

With a focus on mental health and well-being, AnatoME is a powerful tool for emotional healing. Whether you're seeking to understand your emotions better or looking for a creative outlet to express yourself, this book provides a safe and nurturing space for your journey.

Unlock the secrets of your heart and mind, one piece at a time, and emerge from the journey with a renewed sense of self and a deeper appreciation for the beautiful complexity of your emotions. This is a companion for your soul.

A little about me, my memories and my inner child…

My name is Angel, I am an aspiring Psychologist, I love writing poetry, creating art, advocating for mental health, and listening to people. I am also a baker, and an entrepreneur, and opened "Your Sugar Daddy - A Mental Health Cafe," where I combined food and psychology. Here in this book, I am amalgamating art, psychology, memories, and pieces of me. Hope you find pieces of you too.

When I was a kid, I weaved memories in my mind with threads of smiles, snuggles and sometimes tears. A soul with sunflowers in my lungs, I breathed through the flecks of dust in sunlight living in Mumbai. This was the time of my life, thinking about it gives me this rare, nostalgic comfort where I think about this city and the memories it gave me. Mumbai's epic rainfall, for instance, a time when my feet told me that some blades of grass are sharper than the others. A time when the soft, wet mud hugged my feet as I jumped in the rain. It was never cold but the rain changed it, it was as if it resisted change throughout the year, but finally gave in, with a burst of overflowing tears amalgamating with the sea, while the waves laughed at it.

Bombay

This city has some kind of multiple identity disorder. It gives people the spice of Vada Pav under the sun, while their sweat drips with a sip of boiling chai. It's true when I say, 'When life gives you the spiciest red chilli, make the best Vada Pav and eat it.' On the other hand, it provides the serenity of waves laughing at marine drive, while rain touches the lips of a common man, telling him he's special to walk in the rain. It is a city where magic meets dreams.

Although I lived there only for seven years, that too, as a child, I feel like that was the place that gave me life, with smiles or tears. It just watered me in a way rain waters a famine.

Mumbai was me—it cried with its rainfall after resisting for a long time. It really tried to resist but once it was broken, it overflowed with tears about everything that had ever happened to it. It was me when the sun rose each day because no matter how much it tried to live in the dark, it always changed to a lighter shade. It is the city of dreams where some climb the walls of success, while others get lost in the basement trying to push through. It is competitive and harsh but deeply teaches you the essence of all that is life: love, laughter, and family.

It absorbs everything and transforms it into its own, much like a tsunami gulping up the personalities of different people and recreating them into better versions of themselves. It nurtured the 4-year-old in me into an 11-year-old who was heartbroken for nearly two years after leaving this magical city. It has been a wild ride since then, but this city gave me everything, including the best time with my grandparents, lifelong friends who are now in different parts of the world, a locked suitcase with infinite smiles, finger-licking street food, boiling chai, speed-breakers, crooked teeth, skinned knees, Christmases with my grandparents, and everything that I am today.

Write a little about you, your memories and your inner child…

This book begins with darkness, and ends with finding yourself. Hope you enjoy the ride, don't forget to be true to yourself while turning the pages.

Level
1
starting the
puzzle,
dealing with
the broken &
lost puzzle
pieces
anxiety

Cast a w a y

let me peek through my fogged window
where the sunlight tints into my eyes
I close the curtain, hopeless
no one came to see me today.
I am alone, in my room
the rods are dark,
the pillows wrinkled,
untidy bed, scribbled walls,
differentiated my pencils, kept them neatly in
a cage
integrated my clothes, rolled them into my
broken cupboard
the music plays from the mute radio,
when the darkness of shadows frees itself,
through the tiny space at the end of my door,
trying to take me out
but I like this—I like being alone. I would
never want to go out.
the shadows don't leave
the people don't come
being alone is a
blessing
but not so much when your shadow leaves
Too

Describe a place where you feel SAFE & FREE from loneliness. What elements make this place COMFORTING? :)

nature doesn't see blocks

here, stuck between rocks that look like
corals
one headless bark with
no story to write
homeless people are here used as
morals.
there were battery-less torches,
That used to shine bright
It was better when masks didn't filter
our air for us but now,
there are no lights—just an empty
box that has timeless clocks,
inside that shut
our vision, they dim the lights
that are aplenty.
trees crawl down, as if they want to meet you
but the sky is a jacket they don't want
to wear in winters, they will wear jimmy
choo.
this is where the chatter flows,
the water
meets but does not glow, it hates
the people
walking by, wishing they were in the
Sky

draw A map representing where you feel **STUCK** in your life right now. What is the root of this feeling?

Bleached Blood

Unused chandelier candles floating up the
ceiling while
The waves of our huge carpet flow around
the 40x20 feet floor.
Hollow rooms, expensive furniture and
Air. Dust in dawn, void in dusk. Gloom
under the rough
White sheets, waiting to breathe in detergent
Coupled with loads of silverfish searching
for human dirt on the carpet.
Blank canvases hung on walls without
anchors, and
paint cans remain sealed in the
red room. The house is new, but the red is
turning brown
The chandelier screams as the back of the
canvas kisses the wall; it
Craves to be lit, to be touched, but the hall is
abandoned by them. There's
No one around to swim on the carpet or fly
beneath the ceiling,
No one to unseal the paint cans, or attach the
wall anchors,
No one to breathe on the white rough sheets,
and no one to clean the
blood from the
red room.

Fill this room with things that make
YOU FEEL EMPTY...

draw   write   scribble

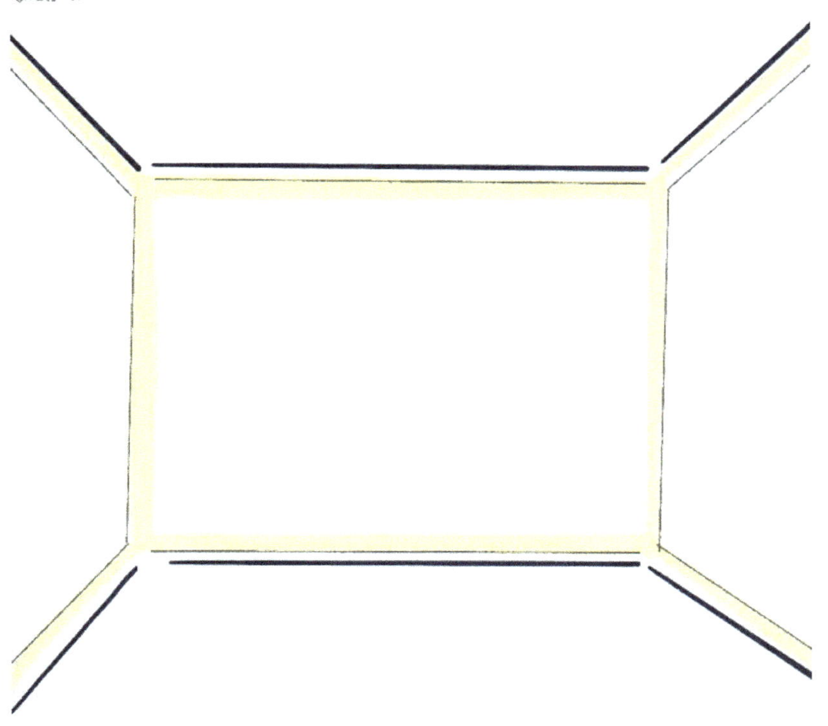

Ceiling crush

A ruptured heart with veins cut through, is now a house with broken
corners, and if the corners are broken, how will the ceiling
Balance.
If a mountain didn't have a peak, how could you
watch a view? There would just be a straight line, where
everyone would see the
same, be in the same
place, at the same level—six feet under.
But to be a home with fixed corners, you must have people
To hold up the ceiling, while you cement the corners.
You must have help, a family
Or the ceiling will crush
You. Don't fear the straight line;
Fear the jump from high to low, the loss of
A loved one when they experience a flat line.
Look for the pain that glorifies my wounds, which are earned and not worn. Hand me a mirror, so that I could look at my wounds, to cherish them.
Don't throw away broken glass, paint
On it, glue it,
Frame it. Be proud of it.

fill in these puzzle pieces with
the different emotions you feel
and what TRIGGERS them.

Topsy-turvy vision

The glass howls
In the inner labyrinth of my ears
While my diaphragm relocates
Ordering my body to slink
Against the numbing mud-ridden squidgy
path.
Tiny mirrors have now
Shattered, as the
Tyres squeal. Blood
Slithers down my
Throat.
It stains my skin
By greasing it with
Red. It is though,
Like kohl.
Something to
Wear with pride.
I can taste
My slimy blood
intertwined with velvety mucus.
With cuts so roomy,
That the bristled
glass pieces
barbed inside my throat
Are now living in me,
Feeling at home.
As if puzzle pieces
Have now settled for

Level 1

the unadorned beauty found in the
Tanginess
of my blood. It comforts them.
algor mortis,
corpse not found.
it's been fifty-seven
years now,
and I can only taste the
the drought in my mud-ridden tongue
with the pieces of bones that lay
beside my
body. It's been
fifty-seven years
and now, the glass pieces have
sold their home
and are living in my bones.

Name these
broken pieces based
on what makes you
feel broken.

and then...
reflect,
COLOUR,
draw,
Scribble
let it out . on this page

Level 1

Dear smile,

it's been a while since I saw you. You're the
cup that hugged my coffee, but my teeth are
now stained. And I don't like you anymore.
I don't like you on my face, my
Eyes like to rain and my teeth
Are always stained
With coffee,
With tears,
With blood.
I am in the
Sun,
Hearing the funniest
Joke, the cutest
Giggle.
My eyes squint,
My nose squishes,
But my mouth clenches.
The eyes are your landlord,
And you haven't paid,
because happiness, your parent,
Isn't here.
so you left to find them.
But it's been two months now.
No songs remind me of you,
Memories have been a tunnel,
Lightless.
Dear smile,
I'm sorry. Even if I carve you

Like the Joker did,
It would not be funny.
Just, the same sadness, with the same eyes,
dominating you.

WHAT DO YOU EMOTIONALLY CRAVE RIGHT NOW? WHAT IS STOPPING YOU FROM FEELING IT?
WHY?

Permanent slumber

The steam in my throat
The everlasting warmth,
Collides with lemon drops,
bit by bit
the aroma invades my soul,
warmth covers up the signs,
and kills me right there.
The steam,
The residue of life.
Now,
Death.

These shells will be eaten by the waves soon. Fill them in with your problems and imagine them flowing away :‑

Lemonade

I go to the beach every day
Where lemons
Are squeezed and doves
Find their way.
The waves are soapy and dark, they crackle
like fire
Naked in the sand, while the mud touches
My lips, drugged with sugar,
Rests the smell of rotten
Egg beside me.
It's a dead body that I killed,
Remember how you taught me, on those
Sunday brunches? To tie up the bodies
And soak them in
Saltwater, remember?
I did the same for you.
You're welcome.

Choose colors that represent how you're feeling today.
Create a simple painting/drawing/scribbling/collage using
these colors.

Murder lesson during brunch

My sole plays with black sand particles
every day, while I crush lemons
In my Earl Grey tea. The waves are
soapy and dark, as if the fish are cleansing
themselves
To be transparent. They are crackling like
fire, though, as if the fish are being cremated
Tiny sips of my tea,
with a dark view.
Naked body in the sand,
With the grittiness resting on my lips.
I eat it,
It tastes just like you did.
My throat is filled with your
Warmth now.
Your soul occupies this space
It moves as I do
I know it because your staleness is in the air
In the sand
And in the water.
On those Sunday brunches,
Remember how you taught me? to tie them
first, soak them in ice and then
bury
their bodies in the black sand,
Where the water is dark
They won't know if it's blood
Or water.

8 Things you feel PRESSURED by:

(fill in the names of these figures)

The Red Paintbrush

The amalgamation of raindrops and the sound on the radio is the perfect lullaby for me. I just woke up and I don't remember anything, my eyes feel parched and I can feel the air resonating sounds in my throat. I feel like the texture of the world around me is stretching, I'm dizzy and it's hard to figure out. This is strange, how did I get here? Oh, alright, Atif is driving, I am safe. But I can't help noticing that his eyes are blood red, he doesn't look like himself and the weather looks so sad. It's been a while since I saw the clouds crying as the lightning stabs through them, the water droplets are scared, they are running down the naked window as I gaze at the piqued sky. The radio is playing *'Ajeeb dastan hai yeh'* and it fits the moment perfectly, because the roads are empty, almost eerie. Maybe this journey will never end.

"Oh, you are up. You look so beautiful, I didn't want to wake you up. We're going to reach the villa in about an hour. I hope my face isn't scaring you—I haven't slept. My eyes are sore from driving nonstop for the past 14 hours," said Atif.

"God. 14 hours, really? Where are we heading though? I don't remember anything after packing Sadia's bag for her art class.

How did we even get here? And where is Sadia? I don't see her Polly Pocket bag; did you leave her at Ammi's?" I asked him, as I saw the lines forming on his forehead. He looked frightened, or rather, shocked.

"Uhm, who is…who's Sadia, sweetheart? And what are you saying? Don't you remember we are driving to Goa for our vacation?" said Atif. I could tell that he was lying.

"What? Is this a joke? Is she hiding under the seat? Did you forget our 4-year-old daughter? What year is it?" I demanded as he abruptly stopped the car.

"Sunshine, I think you're out of your mind. When did we even have a baby? We have yet to plan for one, it's 1989. I think you were dreaming. Too much REM sleep for you, is it? Ha! It's alright. A massage will calm you down when we reach the villa," he said.

"No. You are lying. You're a father. She was born in 1985, she turned 4 two weeks ago. She's the epitome of our love, our entire existence," I insisted.

"Enough of it. If you think we had a baby, don't you remember what Dr. Wadia said? He said you could only have a C-section, not a normal delivery. Now, check your stomach for any scars, I am sure there won't be any. You have been losing your mind, we will deal with all of this when we reach the villa," he said, with his eyes staring into mine.

His hands were trembling and droplets of sweat condensed on his forehead as he spoke.

"I remember Dr. Wadia saying that I had a tiny pelvis and couldn't have a normal delivery. There are no marks, I checked. Uhm, maybe it was a dream, but if it was, it was a darn long one, marked with the essence of reality," I said.

I feel like Pac-Man, trying to digest reality. The bad guys are the fear of confusion in the back of my mind, I know they are coming for me. They will be here soon but all I can do is digest as long as I can. Okay, they are here now. I feel like Atif is lying, but since there aren't any scars, maybe it's me. I am a lost puzzle piece longing to fit in here but feeling alienated since I woke up. My husband feels like the water in a Campa Cola bottle, the interaction we had today had a different kind of intensity to it. Maybe it's the weather, drawing out the coldness inside of us.

We reached the villa in no time. This villa seemed alienated compared to the others, the trees around it were large enough to hide its existence. As we entered it, we noticed there were huge white walls that needed to be climbed, not jumped off. They were like an empty canvas waiting for colours, maybe the colour red? The rooms were airy, allowing the sunlight to enter and touch my bare body when I was in bed. The kitchen had all the required appliances and food resources, it was as though we didn't need to go out of the villa to buy anything. Everything we needed was in front of us. However, it was strange that there was not even a single mirror, not even in the bath.

I hadn't packed my bags, but I found paintbrushes dipped in red inside. I love Atif. He did not forget my paintbrushes, he knew that a painter's pleasure is painting even on vacation. We paint when there's a war inside of us, or when we know the waves are soothing our souls, we can paint every day as our body fights off the world and our brain creates memories.

"Sweetheart, I am sorry if I was rough on you earlier, it was the truth I was introducing you with. There has been no baby, there might be one in the future, but not now. Anyway, I'll have some meetings during this vacation but I don't want you leaving this house, it's unsafe outside. I also want you to avoid mirrors, because I want you to increase your self-confidence and not care about how you look. You have to stay in at all times and enjoy the vacation by taking your mind off everything. You can just paint, but there should be no human interaction, it's healthy. Oh, did you see I got some oil paints for you? I hope you like them," he said with a smile as he entered through the front door with suitcases.

"It's alright, I think it was a silly dream. Maybe the dream was a sign that we should start trying for a baby? I feel like there is a void between us which will be filled by another tiny life. And, I don't mind staying in and painting, alright, no mirrors, it's all up to you, my little psychiatrist. If it's healthy, I trust you completely. You really understand my love for painting, thank you, I love the oil paints. I think it's time for you to get some sleep now, alright?" I said.
"Yes, of course. I will wake up soon, you can paint till then or maybe cook something, but remember, you must not leave the house. You need to stay inside," he said.
"Yes, I will," I nodded.
It was like he demanded all of this. I couldn't say no, he's my husband after all. But is he my husband? I feel like it's someone else. Someone has replaced my husband—someone who looks like him. I wondered why he asked me to stay inside. If it was unsafe for me, why did he rent a villa in this area? Was it just my mind running out of thoughts or was he planning to do something

to hurt me? This villa is far away from civilization, it's in the shadows of the gigantic trees where snakes swirl up. This is frightening, I need to pay close attention to his every move. How does he even have meetings here when we don't know anyone in Goa? He got me paints, does he want me to paint so that I stay busy while he plans something against me? Oh, I will paint. I will show him how I can distract him while he thinks he is trying to distract me. I will harm him with whatever I've got. I will use my paintbrushes.

But for now, I should sleep as well.

It has been up to 4 days since we arrived, and I have only seen Atif blaming me for things I haven't done. I have been following him everywhere, trying to keep track of what he will do to me. Last night, I heard him whispering, and I couldn't help but notice that he was talking to himself in a hand mirror.

"It's been a while since I've talked to anyone besides the love of my life. I have been trying to avoid it, to avoid saying it out loud, even in whispers. I don't want her to be imprisoned. She-she…killed our 4-year-old Sadia. She was just packing her bag, getting a paintbrush for her mother and…her mother poked the paintbrush into her eyes and then snapped her neck. I couldn't believe myself, I didn't sleep for 2 nights and dosed my wife with morphine for 2 days. Had to take care of my little sunshine's body. It was like someone had smashed a glass right into my heart, knowing that my wife killed our child. I just didn't want to lose her too, so I brought her here. But, after I researched her condition, I was made familiar with a disorder I'd never heard of—Capgras Delusion. It's what killed my child and made me lose my wife. My family. I built myself a home with them, they were my doors, my windows, and they let me breathe but now, I am a broken home. When I saw her, she claimed someone had replaced Sadia, and it was not our daughter, which is why she was threatened and ruined our lives by committing that dreadful act. She did not even tear up, not even a bit. She didn't do it, the disorder did it. Now, she doesn't remember anything, I did her a favour by lying to her about not having a daughter and by bringing her here, far away. If she ever finds out, she would never forgive herself. I love her too much to let her kill herself after knowing the truth. I have been hiding you to keep myself sane here. To remind me of the reality and to wreck myself daily. I gave her paints, to help her thoughts heal. I hope she feels better now," he whispered to the hand mirror before hiding it away.

I was painting a red toolbox with dead flowers as a still life when I heard all of this. I remember detailing the flowers when he said 'she killed', uhm but I don't think I did it because, I can't. I don't believe him. Moreover, I think it was the mirror talking. I need to find the mirror and ask questions. After Atif leaves, I will find it and talk to the mirror.

He left. I found the mirror, but I couldn't recognize my reflection. I had nail marks on my cheeks, on my shoulders. Suddenly, I landed into the nightmare I call reality, I killed my child while she was trying to dig her nails into me. I can hear her voice rising and fading into utter silence. I can feel her blood on my face, on my hands. I can feel it, right now. I am not her mother, I am her death. I am supposed to give her life, but I took it instead. This reflection isn't me, someone has replaced me. I need to be punished for letting myself get replaced. I don't deserve to live. I don't deserve to paint, I don't deserve to hold a paintbrush because it's become a weapon. It's the weapon.

Oh no, I see him standing at the front door. He is right here, and he found me with the mirror. But the truth is, it is not him. He has been replaced. I need to finish painting my red toolbox, with my red paintbrush dipped in his blood. As I think about this, I break the hand mirror and slit his neck with the sharp piece of glass in my hand. He cannot breathe, and I find it so satisfying. That's his punishment for replacing my husband. Now, I have nothing to worry about, I can finish painting the red toolbox.

With the same sharp piece in my hand, I say, *"It is my turn, no one can replace me now."*

---

the Man called death

The walls of this asylum are thicker,
I can see the dull yellow stains of mildew in
its purest form,
but when I inhale in front of the walls
they smell. They smell of rotten eggs mixed
with cinnamon
and bones,
as if there are
Dead bodies assembled within
Waiting for the screams to screech out my
thoughts,
so that I can paint myself red,
and taste those rotten eggs,
while the warmth of cinnamon crawls up
my glassy skin.
Do you know
that I see him every morning?
When my muscles are stone rigid, refusing to
create movement
With the bristly bronchioles in my chest,
poking the ventricles of my heart.
I see him in the
corner of my room where
the flecks of dust are
not visible, there's no sunlight to create the
milky way of dust
at dawn
That's where I see him.

His skin is tarnished, wrinkles are resting on
his face creating
perfect parabolas.
Parabolas like the ones in the middle of sea
saws, with giggles
And sunlight, with
Children.
Maybe he's here to take me with him, he
knows
That I stabbed my son,
right in his right ventricle
with my metal paintbrush
oiled in his velvety blood as he squawked
I was there
With a smile on my face.
A perfect parabola on my face.

IMAGINE a
scenario where
you are in your
WORST NIGHTMARE.
How do you face
it? How does facing
this fear change
your perception
of it?

Rooh.

The red is screaming in my throat. A tequila shot in my eyes, with veins popping out.
Ice floor with frozen blood cubes. Walls with mildew, covered with oozing snakes. Slithering. Crawling. Lying. Killing. Oozing. Rue is tie and die.
In my throat, the red screams. Tequila poured into my eyes, popping veins screeching for help. Frozen blood cubes ate blood. Mildew has oozing snakes. Die Rue, tie. Popping throat.
Starving snakes, oozing blood. Rue made frozen blood cubes for tequila. Red is screaming. Eyes frozen. I am tied. Rue is dead. Snakes crackle, blood cubes melt. Mildew sucks the blood. walls scream. Tequila's frozen in my throat. Rue, screeching out for help now. We are tied with snakes. With icy blood tequila poured on us. It's Kasab. Kasab. Kasab. Kasab. Kasab. Kasab. Kasab.
Shot in my eyes. Popped out veins. Kasab killing. Rue and I crawling. Lying. Slithering like snakes. Screams. Thirsty ice. Crackling walls. Terror. Red screams.

Beat your ANxIETY by tracing over these lines:

I am present in this moment and I am safe
My ears listen to what my anxiety has to say.
It is temporary. count the flowers on this page. hold your breath and let it out

Nosedive

overflowing infinities in a box, lips
shackled with battery-less eyes. Colossal
potential to burn, but
no gasoline to chase our
numb bodies, with egos sized as blue
whales, but
attachments are only
meant for emails.
Moulded in boxes, with 2 megabytes
Worth of memories on
The wall. A confined life,
where the eye
views news.
With sleeping masks on, in a
Room without curtains, we ignore
the flecks of
sunlight, trembling in the
gleam. But we do focus
on the screen.
Dreams play in a dead
head while grief
is flushed in the human
cubicle. The wood is now
our bed and walls
are filled with melting clocks.
Time melts every
day, all we are left with is
its residue—the residue named
memories, that fade

away. Skeletons float in the
ocean of tears, while humanity
hangs on chandeliers.
They float and we take a
Nosedive, getting back to another
episode of black mirror.
There's one place for everybody that makes
everything better and everything
safe, this place could be a bedroom or a
grave.

HUMAN
INVASION
ALERT

darkness
i am so excited, i'll get to make friends. it's been lonely.
oh no. darkness is so scary
you

darkness
am i that dark?
you

darkness
you
i'm sorry, darkness.
here, talk to me, take
my hand, i'm
your friend.
i'm here to listen, i'm
here to be there for you.

what? how are you small?
i was small all along, you just kept stretching me.
Thank you for being my friend.
i'll make you shine the brightest
you
darkness

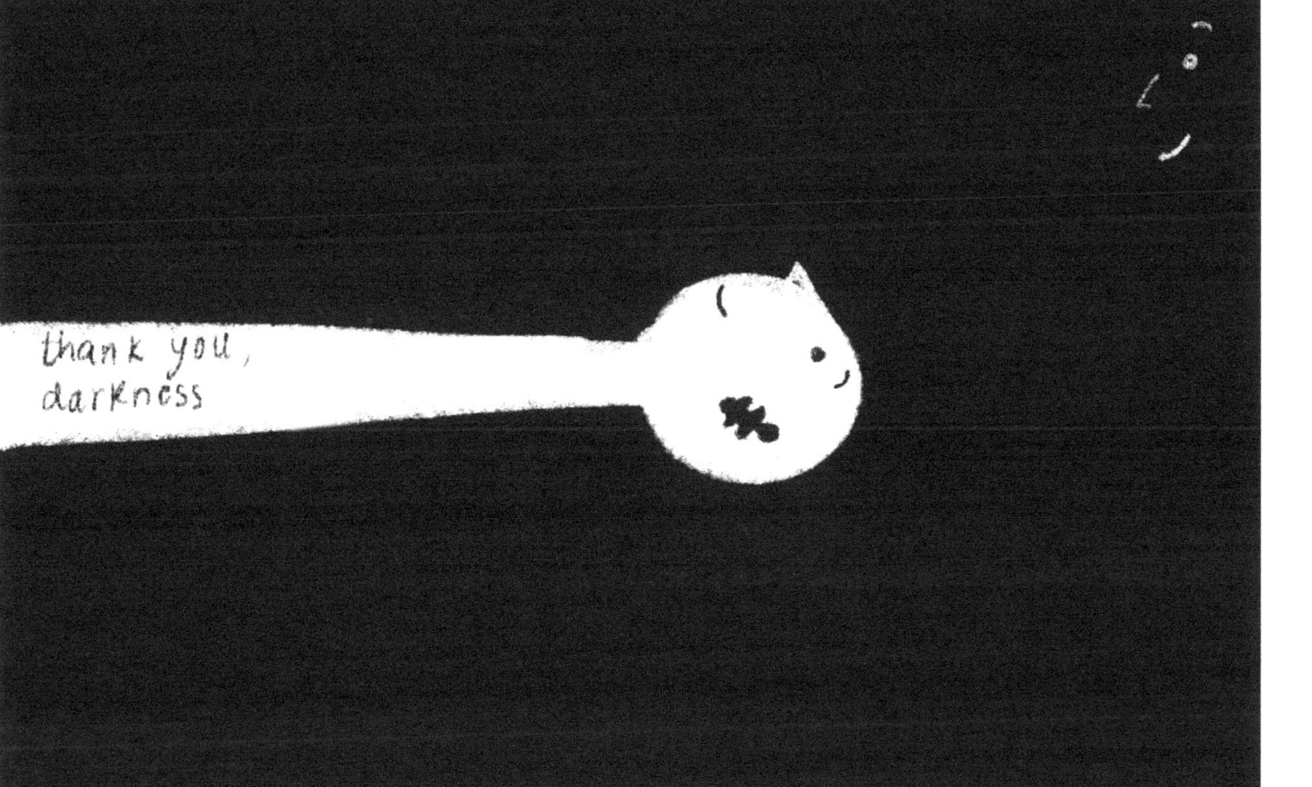

thank you,
darkness

Level2
stitching the
puzzle, finding
your
INNer child

Sad sells

romanticised versions
Of us
On screens
Pages
Surfaces
fleeting moments
tears of sadness,
breakups,
death,
funerals,
sell more.
We smile when we say good morning to a
stranger,
We cry when a close one is in pain.
Sadness needs more effort
Happiness is a butterfly, fluttering by.
But sadness, a tortoise
It's slow yet it wins the race.
be sad
do it, do it right now
think of your worst fear,
imagine it being in front of you
feel sad
until you adjust yourself to the
possibility of it.
once accepted,
it would become tolerable.
it'll sell, but the price would be too high.

sell it for cheap until you have the ability to
increase the price
Of your sadness, your worth and
your smiles.
you cannot find the
Happiest version of yourself until
You meet the saddest one.
be worthy of happiness, be the rainbow,
stand still in the sky
AFTER you have fallen from the sky
and touched the ground being droplets of
rain.

Here's a picture of your healing heart. Inside the heart, write the positive qualities you inherited from your parents.

Level 2

we are ceramics

My mother broke every dish in the house that day except…the ceramic one with my little sister's hand impression on it. Mom had taken ceramic pottery classes to help with the bills, and she decided to do an impression class in which my sister participated. Sara painted a thousand-watt smile on her face as she pressed her tiny hands onto the ceramic plate. This was when my little sister was here, alive. Those days with wet pillows, broken glass pieces beside her white bed in her airy room with flowing white curtains, those midnights when she retched out blood on the floor, and her voice would break as she howled. The days our eyes turned into cameras, capturing memories worth a thousand terabytes.

This plate was special. It was an unbreakable one, but she broke us when she left. My father left before that, he called it 'hospital bills for chemotherapy,' but we called it 'her last days with us.'

'Could you get me some chocolate ganache you made for my birthday cake? I want my mouth to hug it like teddy hugs me,' these were the last words, she conveyed with her dry voice. I ran with a sprained foot to the fridge which was a thousand metres from her room.

My hands were muddy in chocolate by the time I returned. It was raining and droplets covered my face as I rushed into the hospital and bolted my way to her room. She had left, and rain droplets weren't the only thing that made my eyes wet.

ANY ADVICE YOU WOULD LIKE TO GIVE YOUR YOUNGER SELF?

what was she made for

her hair was neatly braided
when her mom left her at their place
they gave her warm food, the TV remote too
didn't check on her much,
but their son did, who wasn't very big
she was merely four,
and he was about thirteen.
He would play with planes, rocks, boards
and Barbies
the plane could fly,
and rocks could roll
dices that could break
but the Barbie would mould
the mould wouldn't go away,
even after colouring her red,
burning the messy hair,
or by scraping the head
the skin would stick, the feet would
be upright.
all her dresses, all her styles,
ruined in the blink of an eye.
the mould always stayed, smelled, and
increased over time, it reminded her
that Barbie will never recover, she would
always be the
chosen character to play the lead in
The mime.

THIS IS THE PAGE OF Secrets, you can wish, dare to reveal the truth or just write your deepest secret(s)!
REMEMBER TO USE A LIGHT COLOURED MEDIUM :)

Catch me dad

I jumped into the pool
of glimmering water with tiny squares,
It was made to make room for me.
The water slithered onto
My petite shoulders
My hair, soaked in chlorine.
Itchy swimsuit
Itchier face, wearing a smile with
Crooked teeth.
Perfect teeth, dead hair, not an itch,
but slithering tears.
standing on a cliff, staring into the
Unknown.
sunlight playing with the tiny green trees on
the mountain.
Wishing I could play, but it's time to pay,
It's better
To fall.
"Catch me, Dad."

Recall a time your parents really listened to you. How did it impact your relationship?

if they haven't listened to you even after you've tried, act like your parent and listen to yourself. :)

When I was a kid,

I waited for my dad to come home from work so that I could climb up on his arms in the air and swing, as if sky diving in the Spanish skies. It was an era of carefree smiles and twinkling eyes that came alive with a bite of McDonald's McVeggie. The flavour dripped down the lips of a 7-year-old, who was enveloped in mayonnaise while she was being fed by her hero.

But the flavour turned into poison when she heard her parents screech out their anger at each other, on the other side of her wall. She scribbled circles on her wall with crayons, hoping for the voices to go away. Little did she know that before the voices would fade away, she'd turn into a grown woman replaying these memories. Memories that are her reality now. I am her.

**Imagine an alternate universe where everyone has an inherent
understanding and empathy for mental health struggles.
How would this change your interactions and feelings?**

Level 2

lmb of memories

I polish a purple popsicle on my teeth
till it makes them numb
I am waiting for Ma and Pa to get on
The bus, but I am a ruptured lung. Because
they are battery-less torches
Lost in a forest at night. I want to be the
firefly that guides
Them, somewhere near me.
But I'm rather a colourless crayon,
While they are a pressed sheet of white
paper.
They screech out their thoughts while I
Howl for help but then, they turn into a
cluttered pair of
wires, placed neatly on a shelf. I've seen
knives that slit
Their tongues, and ropes that
Can pause their breaths,
helping them dig six feet under. But I haven't
seen
a blender.
So I take them with me, on the bus, to
an art gallery. So that I can be a 1GB USB
with more
than 1mb of memories. I want them to

57

know that I can enter the
Starry Night, independently. I want them to
believe
That this is no broken home, it's a death
penalty. But will
They cry for me, and not for each other,
when I'm gone? When they
can't find another blender? Will they cry
when I go inside
The Starry Night?

I saw it rain after dancing with
the Blues and the moon-
yellow hues, I see them looking
at me with regret, as I
wave from the moon.
I wonder if the rain
Made their eyes wet.

EVER FEEL LIKE GETTING LOST? IF YOU GET A CHANCE TO LEAVE, WHERE WOULD YOU GO FIRST?

The sun

On the days when the sky is white, there is someone
Who turns the colourless ocean blue.
He is on a boat from dawn till dusk, with an
Unlimited can of blue paint,
Painting the ocean. No food, no cap, while the
Heat kisses his black hair, he is here with just an unlimited can of
Paint. Painting all day.
He paints the entire ocean,
But she only notices the blue on the tip of the shore. As his sweat contributes to the salt in the ocean
Water, she sips an iced lemonade under an umbrella.
Her heart is like one of the rocks found at the shore, a rock with no meaning, just a pastel appearance waiting to be
Complimented. While the boy paints,
The woman blames him for making the water too blue,
She likes it colourless—
Just like her life.

you've got this, you can help them. :)

the elder wand

doors are slightly shut,
while the mind boils
Throats are internally cut,
while their body coils.
The elder one
Matures through pain,
Not
Age.
screaming is prohibited,
teary eyes are best friends with guilt.
voiceless whines are
like yawns,
normal, compelling them to sleep.
taking everything in, being the hand that
helps,
doesn't ask for it, doesn't scream, doesn't
show. Pillows are wet, dreams are burdened
With responsibilities,
almost parenting.
some sort of artwork they created is present
too,
standing in the gallery, it's reciting the poem
they wrote.
Matilda is present too, asking you about your
Parents. You say they are here,
they aren't bad.
they're just humans.

Here's a tree, put in your family's inter generational traumas instead of naming the members. Would you pass these on?

When I was a kid

I was searching for the sun, on a monotonous day. However, I had lost it forever. When I heard the news, a single tear gave way to an ocean of misery. "He's no longer with us." The words rang in my head as I sat down and tried to register what had happened. My grandfather, as bright as the sun, had left us with the crying skies. I had not seen him in a long while; which is one of my biggest regrets. The wisdom he passed on and the blessings he bestowed upon me not only resonated with me, but also consumed me; they filled my mind every time I cooked, even though he wasn't here dancing with a glass of Old Monk in honey water.

His passion, the ability to make one smile, with that twinkle in his eye, could make a person standing on land, transfer onto quicksand, melting away in a conversation with him. His compassion always motivated me; it gave me an insight into how a curve on a face gives meaning to life. The positivity he generated was to be kept safe. Memories aren't something that can be downloaded in the form of pictures, rather they are vivid snapshots, flashbulb moments that can only be replayed.

As I reminisce the memories of my grandfather, I can't help but remember my grandmother who went to him after 5 years. My saliva used to evaporate on her double-jointed fingers as I jumped from one sofa to the other while she ran after me, with food in her hand. Our broken conversations intertwined as she put three strands of my hair over one another, creating a perfect space for ties and clips to hug my hair.

You know what else I miss a lot? The food. I still remember the warmth of the boiled rice on the stovetop over my 7-year-old face, the aroma of fish curry mixed with coconut and garam masala that lit up the fireflies in my heart during Sunday lunches with my grandparents. Nothing could compare to her joy when she helped her grandparents cook coconut fish curry.

These stories aren't really sad, you know? They always take a turn to the dead end, crashing upon a lane of honeyed memories interweaved with love. I do get overloaded with sad flashbacks worth 1TB, but they're all put to trash when their smiles become my desktop wallpaper.

I wish they could see me today, I cook and bake on my own. I wait for their taste buds to rest under the strawberry cream cheese licked off of my special red velvet cupcakes. A person with a heart can drive a truck 20 miles every day. If I calculate this into an average person's lifetime—equivalent to a journey to the moon and back. When I say I love my grandparents, my dada dadi, to the moon and back, I mean that I love them with all the blood my heart pumps throughout my life.

Car ride away from home

fermented rice batter,
crushed coconut, grounded coffee.
caramel hands, and a gold tooth.
the golden smile says good morning, it's
getting late.
not taking a moment to say
Goodbye,
just because I thought I'd meet them again.

Eclipsed onion

The onion peels itself
As the spice in the air reaches her eyes
Her eyelashes crave the touch of oxygen, but
they only get
sodium chloride
dripping, flowing, streaming.
The cornea is protected
By basal tears

The onion peels itself
Breathing, waiting to be cubed
While the almond eyes
suffocate, waiting for blindness

Her eyes
Are now
drowning in the sweetest nectar

But the day before the full moon
Her eyes fought the discomfort of kohl
leaving,
colouring her crescent under eyes in the
Perfect shade of black.
This was the day her eyes bid her
body
Goodbye

The wood burnt itself
As the spice in the air reaches her eyes

Her eyelashes crave the touch of oxygen, but
they only get
sodium chloride
brimming, burning, blurring,
the loss of her child.
The cornea is protected
By tears
But she is
Dismantled.

We have lost a person, family, relationship, job, money, love, life, future, present, past, time, pet, energy, will, motivation, emotions, and much more, or nothing. Draw or describe how your grief would look as a person, animal or a thing. Caress it, cry with it. Grief is just all the love that was unexpressed. You've got this. You can heal :-)

Level 2

beginning to forget you

You've been dead for a while now.
I use the Shazam tool on the song stuck in
my head, the one that you used to sing
But there's an error
not in my memory.
I am losing your voice in my head
But the song.
The damn song.
Needs to get out
Needs to be played
It is the prayer, the beat,
The rhythm
Of our bond.
It is the paper cut that never dries,
It is the strength of a single hair tie
With two knots that you made, and the
Shiny yolk of the egg that fades.
It is what I can go back to,
Because I can't hear you breathe anymore, I
can only hear the beat, but the song is
missing.

Curate a playlist of songs that resonate with
your feelings and offer comfort.
Put them on the vinyl sleeve, use all the space
you need it is your book.

SONGS THAT GET YOU THROUGH THE DAY:

Level 2

Loosened Rosary

I have forgotten how
it felt to be in the vicinity of you, sleeping
beside me. But I remember the coldness of
my saliva on your fingers, while
you fed me after I came home from school.
I have
forgotten the colour of your
rosary. But I remember how
you prayed for my health, while
I blended my thoughts into pillows before
sleeping.
I have forgotten
whether I enjoyed annoying you as I
jumped from one square foot to the couch, to
the table and impersonated
Mowgli. But I remember
the tightness of your hugs, just like
beach sand envelops the feet. I have
forgotten the last
time I thought about you. But I remember
the last words you said.
I have forgotten
the wetness of
rain on my clothes, as I jumped into shallow
puddles. But I remember
the radiance of your room reflecting

on your smile, with your eyes fading into
sunlight.
I have forgotten the pattern
on your clothes the last time I saw you,
But I remember that
I will never see you again.

Imagine planting a garden with 5 flowers. Each of them represents a cherished memory of your loved one. What memories would each flower hold?

you
Oh my! Are you the infamous HAPPINESS!? I've been trying to get an appointment with you since so long! what happened? why are you so small? Where are your arms?
uhm. yes. hello there. I am indeed. Sorry, I can't speak much, I am really burnt out.
happiness

you
there, there.
don't worry.
I am patient
enough to meet
you and listen to
what happened to you
so tell me...
uhm, okay.
everyone fights
to have me. ALL
OF THEM want me.
but when they reach
me for their
appointment, they
are not satisfied.
they always hold on
so tight that they break
a piece of me...
happiness

...and the worst part is...even after breaking and getting a piece of me... they don't take it along. They just throw it on the way. They don't feel happy with the little things, they want me as a whole. Why don't they get it? Only when they take a piece of me, only when they actually feel happy & not pretend, only if they don't throw me on the way, will I be able to live with them. They have to share me.

i will never throw your pieces.
i will take them with me.
i will find my happiness in
little things...

you've cracked
the code...
my cracks will
disappear and i will grow
i hope everyone is
like you...
Thank You...

You can find yourself
Level 3
just keep turning your pages :)

FILL THIS PAGE
WITH YOUR
HAPPIEST
memories
don't think much, just write.

Perry

So I related to
This character in
this movie.
They were passionate
Enough
To take a bus, a train, walk on the grass
Paint the Starry Night?
Walk on glass
Barefoot.
With hues of red,
Meet poetry in their dreams
Daydream in their bed.
About this one thing
That was
Mystifying. For them
It was like
When the paint meets the paper, the foot
meets a piece of glass
The ink meets a leaf,
The moon meets
The sun. It's when
Something made them
Feel
Like they breathed the purest form of
oxygen.
But in that movie,
Right before the end,
The character
shot themself.

because they dreamed
while they were trapped in a
cage.
The thought of freeing
Themselves took so much effort, that using a
gun was made
Easy.
And I realised that was not me.
This poem
Will get me out.
It'll make me feel, like the snake
That bites its own tail. Lonely,
But complete.

Did you ever crave freedom as a child? **Reflect** on moments in your life where you have felt most liberated.

What obstacles prevent you from feeling free now? How can you cultivate a sense of freedom in your daily life?

if you met your 7-year-old self, what would
you ask them? what advice would you
want, what would you like to learn from them?

My grandfather's father

I think he spent a fortune
On his favourite biscuit,
Or he might have liked to
Play tennis.
he could have also liked the winter sun,
or maybe the monsoon wetness.
He would have loved to paint,
like I do.
Or maybe, he would have had fun cycling.
he was buried, or burned,
with friends and family of his time.
after they faced all kinds of pandemics,
Wars,
Tears.
they've been dead for a while now,
but I don't know where they are,
I haven't known them.
Like my great-grandchildren,
Won't know me.

family
fame
good health
success
wealth
money
happiness
soul food
confidence
life satisfaction
love

it's raining things that are unlimited for you, but you can only choose 2. what would you choose & why?

There is someone who truly hurt you, someone who didn't apologise. They left you broken. But on this page, you will let them go. You will forgive them. Use this page to write an imaginary letter which you will practice in reality.

Dear ______________

You were a learning lesson. Thanks.

CLOSE
AWAY
MET EACH OTHER
AWAY
TOGETHER UNTIL TIME
INTERRUPTS THEM.

Close your eyes and imagine a *fanTasticAl* world where anything is possible. Describe this world in detail—what does it look like, who lives there, and what adventures would you have? How can you nurture your imagination as an adult?

Write a letter to your puzzled emotions as if they were a friend. Offer them advice and support, and see how this changes your perspective.

Dear Puzzled Emotions,

I love all of you. ♡

Write about your emotions in the form of a mini weather forecast with the past season's explanation.

Are there storms, sunny spells, or cloudy areas?

Predict the coming emotional weather and season, and prepare for it.

Life itself.

A paintbrush has bristles that are the
bronchioles of its lungs,
breathing. This one is rustic, worn.
Used for years, has seen me
toothless,
Then wired in braces,
And now, free.
A journey with the black drops stuck
on its body. Proud, with metal between its
Bristles and its end. This rustic paintbrush is
my
Mother, painting my life through.
I've been holding her while she holds
Me. The metallic superimposition masks
Her worries with a parabola on her face.
She has responsibilities numbered more than
the strands of her
Hair, but she is not
Afraid to dip them in paint.
To live them, and to feel the aroma of the
pungent oil,
In a room full of art.
Where she is the real masterpiece.

Track 1

Track 2

Track 3

Track 4

Track 5

Track 6

Track 7

Track 8

Track 9

Track 10

If you could make 3 wishes come true, they would be:

Alright. So I befriended darkness, I felt happiness, but...

I can't find myself...my authenticity. Me. Where am I? Where is my piece? Where is my peace?

the first song you learned
your handwriting
your favourite childhood toy. your first best friend, the time you fell from the see-saw, your favourite book, warm food on a rainy day. the DVDs you've watched. your laugh. the time you got your ears pierced. when you went to see the movie alone in the theatre. your favourite colour, the sunlight on your face, the wind in the trees, the feeling in a hug. the smile you get after rewatching your comfort movie. the postcard your best friend sends. the times you've clapped for others. everything around you that is beautiful.

Level 4
I FOUND ME...
you   will
                 too...

TO ALL THE PEOPLE

All the emotions you feel are valid.

They are influenced by someone's tone, their way of speaking, their actions, your own actions, experiences, people, death, birth, weather, food, hunger, clothes, colours, books, the sun, the waves, the moon, the stars. 8.1 billion people in the world. 8.1 billion souls, each one of them feel differently every single day, and we all manage to co-exist. Just remember to co-exist while being kind, because there are 8.1 billion emotions in the air right now

I hope you are kind enough, I hope
you are mindful enough. An act
of kindness could change someone's
mood for a second, a minute, an
hour, a day, a week, a month,
a year, their life. It could

change their perception which could

lead to change in others' perceptions.

You are a part of the chain

reaction. You are the world.

DON'T FORGET THAT.

Cycle

Child cried for the mother's love
And she cried for her own mother's love
And she, for Hers.
Her love was distributed in the clothes the
child
Washed,
in the scars drawn on the child's
Face,
In the dried rotis,
In the labour that was taught,
In the silenced cries.
But Her love cycled on,
It was timeless.
Until it ended when
The
Child
Grew
Up
To be
A woman who stopped
Cycling.

Warmth

The warmth you feel when you see your mum smile, is like a field of sunflowers blooming on a sunny day
The warmth you feel when you're watching your favourite movie and your eyes tear up, your nose is almost dry, your throat aches for a breath, and you really need to cry
The warmth you feel when you walk on the scorching sand on the beach, grasping for the ocean to touch your feet
The warmth you feel when a body hugs you tight, it makes your lungs flushier the tighter it gets, the arms wrapped around form a tornado of safety
The warmth you feel in nostalgia, thinking about your school gate opening, blowing out candles on your birthday while your friends cheer for you, or the sound of chimes in your childhood room
Remember this warmth when you're alone, remember it when you need someone, remember it every day, because you need to be warm within to fight the cold outside.

Change

When you grind sugar cubes in a mixer, they heat up to form granules.

You put pressure on them to change, it takes less time but heats them up, which may damage the sugar for future use. Similarly, in life, do not pressurise cubes to turn into granules; they will eventually become granules once mixed with the right environment.

Environment

Sugar cubes don't have an issue mixing with tea, but they do when it comes to a cold glass of milk, you really need to shake them up for a while to mix them up, they take much more time to dissolve than granulated sugar.
Everyone has different capacities in different circumstances—granulated sugar may easily mix in with hot or cold milk, but cubes don't carry the same ability.

Time

Take as much time as you'd like, but don't forget to mix, otherwise, the milk would be tasteless.

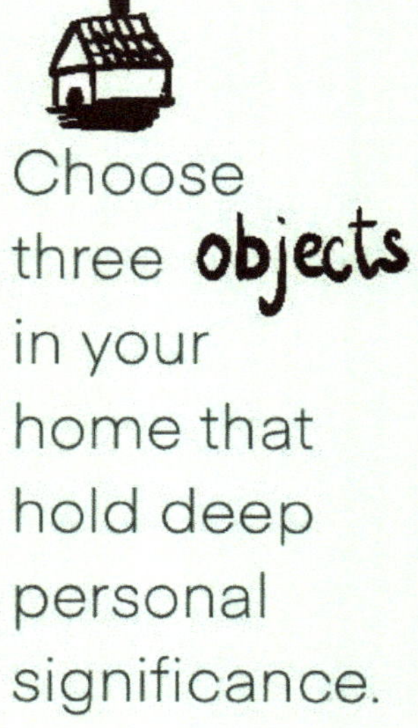

Choose three **objects** in your home that hold deep personal significance.

Describe their importance and how they reflect aspects of your identity.

As kids we usually coloured outside the lines, it was so freeing to just create without worrying about perFECTiON. Think about 3 ways in which we can embrace our imperfections & make our inner child happy again :)

The Duckling's Duck

the perfect pair.
The nail to my painting,
carried the weight of acrylics, oils, water,
glass,
coins, gold,
stress.
the strength was unimaginable.
hanging by the edge, the painting
almost fell,
to the floor, and then she'll be hung to
another
Nail.
Or destroyed.
the nail always caught her,
through attention, concern,
care. A lot of care.
she hung every single day, during
earthquakes, cracks,
But
people praised the strokes,
The hues, glazing,
impasto,
the coins, the gold, the
layers. From primary colours
To secondary,
To textures, and mixing. The nail was always
There.
The strength of the nail went
unnoticed,

While the painting got all the compliments.
The nail was everything:
strong, stuck, had nothing to gain,
only to lose.
lose her strength, her wisdom, her time,
until the wall collapses.
The painting would never be a painting, if it was
Not for the nail.

Here's an open first aid kit, name these items as strengths and coping mechanisms passed down through your family.

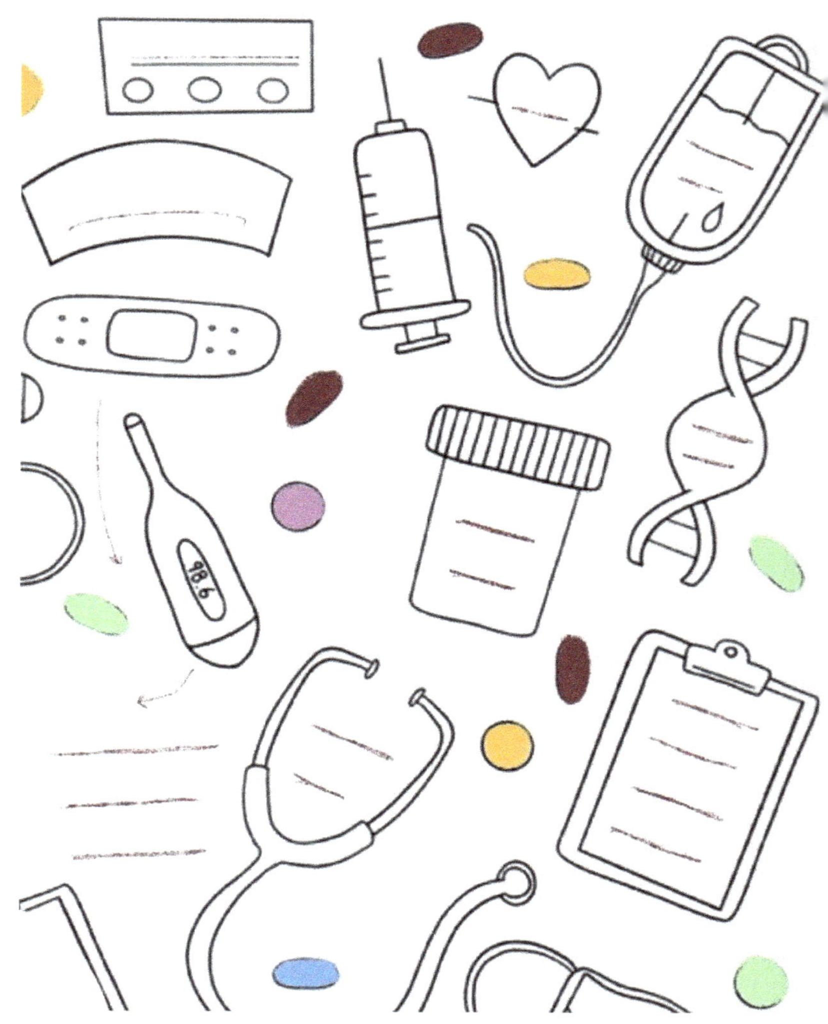
you are strong, you have these
traits :)
98.6

Research the meaning and origin of your
name

Reflect on how your **name** and any nicknames you've
had over the years contribute to your identity.

Your Name: ________________________________

Coconut Moons

astral projection traps me in
a dream where I sew
memories onto sheets of
distances between you and me.
I'm a burning
Fireplace at the end of the
Street. You can't inhale my
Warmth when
you have a runny nose. Your taste buds can't
ever
rest under the fresh
Chocolate ganache I make.
you have not
laid your eyes on my oozing
acne, or on my wrinkly
forehead while I scroll through
infinite posts that do not
feed me. Feed me like you used to.
I remember how
My saliva on your double-jointed fingers
used to turn cold as I
hopped from one square foot to the couch, to
hanging on the
lights. Impersonating Mowgli
with lips ridden in
mango pulp, and eyes
giggling looking at you, running to get a
hold of me.
these snippets

of memories
are like the moments I woke up
feeling the aroma of cinnamon rolls and
coconut moons
on Christmas mornings, with
you. They are like the
lullabies you sang for me while
counting the beads in your
rosary.
The aroma wakes me up, but
I fall asleep to the melodies.

stitched heart, teared eyes

dragging my pen across paper,
making words that don't make sense.
wearing a shoe without its aglet,
slipping out, skinning my knee.
tired of broken noodles,
knitting a sweater with chopsticks,
with needles dug into my head.
washing my face with boiling water,
volcano oozing on my skin,
wearing an incomplete sweater in sweat.
The needles in my head didn't prick.
it had been a while, living with a
numb heart.
every morning, I begged for sleep
every night, I prayed for tears
but the numb heart never gave in.
then you came and
my pen danced on paper,
it wrote poetry, songs, stories, lives.
found my aglet,
and the perfect bowl of ramen.
the volcano was now underwater,
and winter was here, with a complete
sweater.
the needles left, the hair grew back,
my ears grew flowers, as you watered me
with your voice.
the heart finally melted

the ice; the water finally flowed.
dehydrated eyes were now filled,
with tears of everything.

WHEN TIME IS CRUSHING YOUR
SOUL, THE BAND-AID THAT HELPS
YOU HUG THE PIECES, KEEP THEM
TIGHT, IN A BOWL, WARMING
THE ENTIREITY OF YOU, IS YOUR
FAVOURITE MEAL.
Your comfort,
something that fixes
your soul, through
your STOMACH.

what is it?
DRAW, WRITE, FEEL

happiness

this mirror is now,
packed tight,
somewhere safe.
with the secrets, the friendship,
the heartbreak, the tears, the number of times
cried, the river of kohl, expensive mascara,
the stress,
the laugh of the soul.
and the timeline that lived in front of it.
growing, surviving like pieces of chess
being half of what we are now, or maybe
even less.
From curls to straight to curls to braids,
The number of summers, winters, autumns,
springs, the times when the heater cast a
yellow glow on your face.
When the bowl hugged the soup, and the
popsicle melted. The time when the fan
moved at its pace.
The mirror stayed, for a long while
Before it was packed in a
Coffin.
Just to be out, after a while
In its true self,
Gazing at life. Once again.

fill in these
rings with
the people &
things that make
you feel like
a RAINBOW

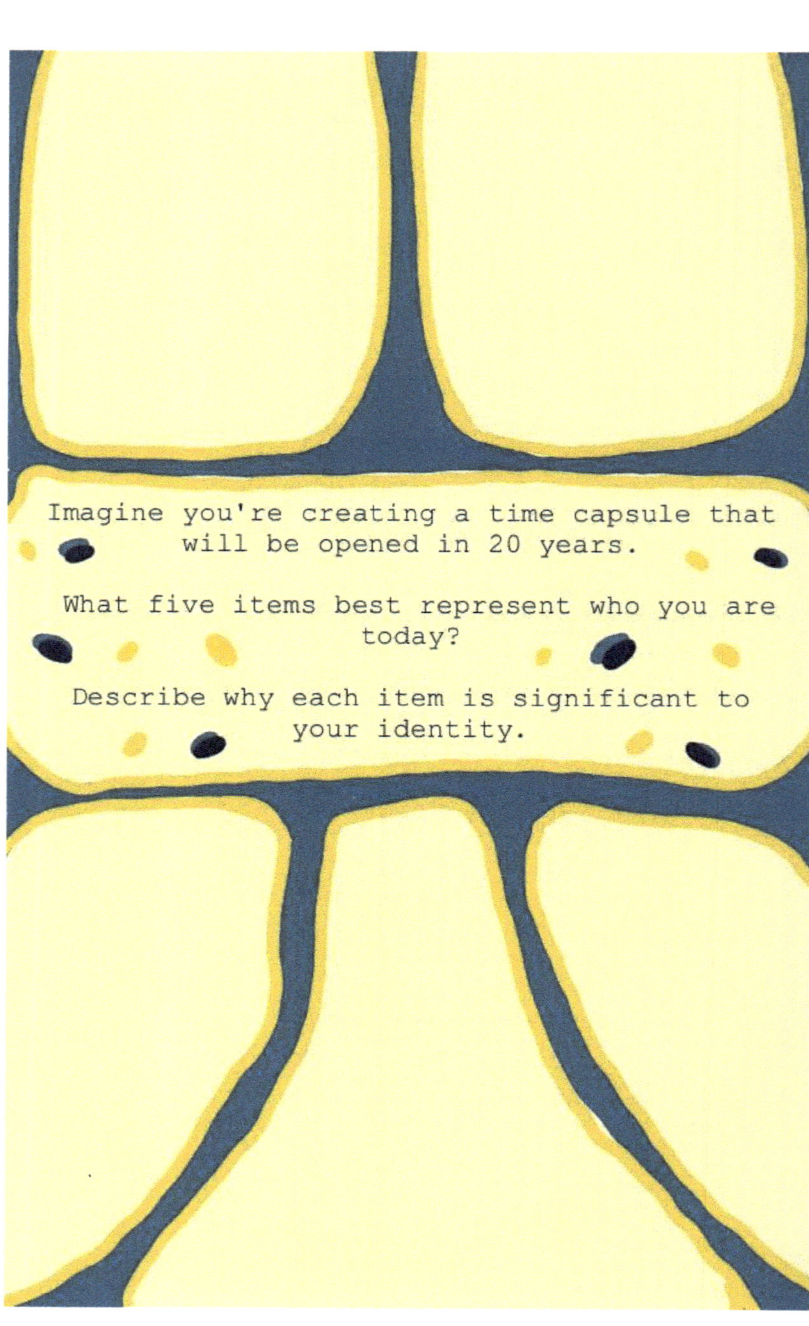

Imagine you're creating a time capsule that will be opened in 20 years.

What five items best represent who you are today?

Describe why each item is significant to your identity.

Imagine your **BRAIN** as a space with different compartments for each emotion. Which compartment is overflowing or stuck?

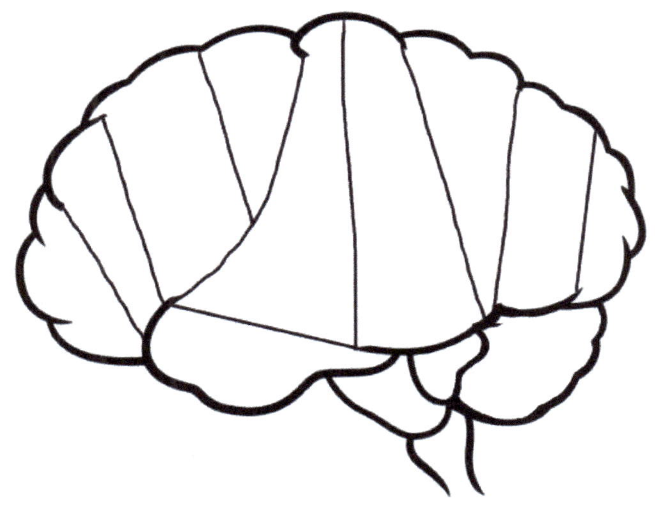

How can you organize or unlock it?

Level 4

The Gold that chose me

the screeching in my breath wakes
me up, he sees it
I pretend I gasp, and sleep.
he saw that.
From
One corner of the bed to the corner of the
floor, eyes meet.
expressions are exchanged,
wishes come true.
tail wags, he's jumping now.
Cannot sleep again.
He's waiting for me to get up,
and I do.
I grab my blue tote bag with a yellow flower
on top, which is the indicator of our
Walk.
He's now running in circles, with that smile.
Gold.
the sunlight runs in, the dust dances.
we walk in the heat, the cold,
the spring, the autumn.
through acne,
scars, tears,
grief of the past.
His eyes do the talking,
his fur does the comforting.
his hair flies, mixes with the universe,
wishing it reaches back to me when I need it
the most.

but no one around me understands what he
means to me,
because they've simply never experienced
the purest form of love.
without words, without expectations, just
simple,
Pure, beautiful love.
with scratches, rubs,
a real amount of patience, and work.
The real gold, the real treasure.

What's something that comforts your inner child?

Sunday

How many times
Would you remember a certain afternoon
Of your
Childhood?
Once, twice, thrice? That's it.
And this is one of those happy Sunday
Afternoons
No school, just you.
Sunshine, or rain,
Your favourite cartoon talking to
You.
Your favourite toy, your favourite pencil,
Your favourite crayon.
It's you.
Do you remember that child?
That afternoon is a particle
Of your existence, it's what makes you
You
Today.
You cannot perceive your life without it.
That afternoon, today's morning,
Tomorrow's night. All paused, for the moon
To rise.
How many times would you see a full moon?
60? Maybe 600?
And if you're lucky, a whole
Lifetime.
But you are lucky, if you are reading this.
Make something of your life,

Appreciate it. Remember the afternoons,
And reflect on your nights,
Make your days brighter
With the sun on your face,
Your own smile.

Create a vision board for your future self. Include images, words, and quotes that represent your dreams, goals, and the person you want to become :-

(ALL THE BEST. YOU'VE GOT THIS)

LIFE TIME

I was really inspired by an art piece that I had seen, so I tried to create my version of it. The artwork reflects on the lifetimes we've lived with a variety of beings that enter, leave, come back, stay close, die, never see us, break our hearts, make us laugh, and much more. It indicates the different relationships we have shared whether it is with our friends, strangers, neighbours, pets, parents, grandparents, teachers or anyone.

We are just a part of our parents' and grandparents' lives, we've been there halfway, but they have always been there, at least in some cases if not all. Our pets only get to share a few years of our lifetime. Our lovers come and go—some stay, some leave. People die and are reborn in alternate universes, where they meet us again. Our friends are here, sometimes they are not. People come, touch your life, leave an imprint on your soul, and leave. Some of them scratch your soul and you have to push them away, while others stay.

Level 4

Some readers might not grasp the essence of this book or its artworks, especially this one. You began an adventure when you opened the book and laid your eyes on the words that created themselves. You wrote, you drew, you imagined, you cried, you smiled, you felt. That was my mission—to make you feel. I really hope you met your inner child, if not met, then you at least tried to find them, and you know they are there.

This world is free, it is full of you, you are everywhere, but most importantly, the world is inside you. Don't forget that you are on a journey, to find yourself, to feel your emotions, to be alive. You are. And you will be.